PENETRATION

Editorial Cartoons and Caricatures
by The Chronicle Herald's Bruce MacKinnon

The 25TH ANNIVERSARY COLLECTION

Foreword by Peter Mansbridge

The
ChronicleHerald NIMBUS PUBLISHING

DEDICATION

For Mom.

Nimbus Publishing Limited

3731 Mackintosh Street,
Halifax, NS B3K 5A5
(902) 455-4286   nimbus.ca

Printed and bound in Canada

Cover and interior design: Heather Bryan

Library and Archives Canada Cataloguing in Publication

   MacKinnon, Bruce
   Penetration : Bruce MacKinnon cartoons : 25th anniversary
   collection / Bruce MacKinnon.
   Co-published by: The Chronicle Herald.

   ISBN 978-1-55109-779-4

1. Canada—Politics and government—2006- —Caricatures and cartoons.
2. Canada—Politics and government—1993-2006—Caricatures and cartoons.
3. Canada—Politics and government—1984-1993—Caricatures and cartoons.
4. World politics—1989- —Caricatures and cartoons. 5. Canadian wit and humor, Pictorial. I. Title.

NC1449.M225A4 2010   971.070207   C2010-903054-0

We acknowledge the financial support of the Government of Canada through the Book Publishing Industry Development Program (BPIDP) and the Canada Council, and of the Province of Nova Scotia through the Department of Tourism, Culture and Heritage for our publishing activities.

CONTENTS

FOREWORD

There's a very strange feeling that goes through your mind when you see yourself portrayed in a Bruce MacKinnon editorial cartoon. A series of feelings really. First, you're flattered. *Wow, he actually drew ME!* is usually the first thought, and you feel all pumped up and somewhat self-important. But trust me, that doesn't usually last too long. Because the next feeling is *I don't really look like that! Do I?* Then it crosses into *How could he do that to me? He's made me come off like an idiot!* And then, sadly, you sneak off into some lonely corner and say to yourself, *Yikes, maybe he's right!*

Bruce has an amazing talent: the ability to imagine a moment in the life of a story—a moment that may only play out inside the chambers of his incredible mind—that captures what the story is really all about. When he puts it on paper, his audience is not only informed, it's enthralled.

At a time when newspapers are being challenged to justify their existence in a media landscape that is changing almost by the day, the editorial cartoon stands out as a truly unique feature. It's the combination of talented art and intelligent journalism. In Canada we are lucky to have many editorial cartoonists who are at the top of their trade, and Bruce MacKinnon has been one of that select group for decades.

When you enjoy the voyage through the pages of this book, keep that in mind—one of the country's most talented journalists is your tour guide to the stories and events that have helped shape us as Haligonians, Nova Scotians, Maritimers, and Canadians. And we should be pretty thankful to have had the pleasure.

Peter Mansbridge
April 2010

INTRODUCTION

As I scribble this down on a March day in 2010, I find myself on the cusp of an unnerving milestone in my career. It's been nearly 25 years since I started drawing a daily editorial cartoon for The Chronicle Herald. The nice folks that make the important decisions at the paper thought it would be a good idea to mark the occasion in some way. While I'm pretty certain I don't rate any special recognition for stamina—any more than the office coffee machine, anyway—it did briefly get my imagination going. Briefly.

"Hmm. Well…25 is the silver anniversary, isn't it?" I asked.

"How about a book?" they replied.

"Oh," I said. "A silver book? You want to give me a silver book?"

"No, no, how about you write another book? Only this time you actually do some *writing*. You know, tell people about what you do—how your day goes, the challenges you face, that kind of thing."

My first reaction was that for most people, reading about my average day would probably rate up there with reading the manual for the new automatic dishwasher or doing their taxes. Recognizing the imminent prospect of more work, I thought some gentle resistance might be warranted.

"But really, y'know, if people are anything like me, they only want to look at the pictures."

"People are nothing like you, Bruce."

"Oh."

So I'm "writing" this book. (Not my forte, but I'm already pretty impressed with myself because I've used the word "forte" in the book I'm "writing.") What follows is a bit of background, some insights, some mindless rambling, a few total fabrications, and a brief look at the pluses and minuses of the profession. Yes, there are minuses. Not the least of which is knowing hundreds of thousands of people are going to see and evaluate my work every day and, if I do it properly, a fair number of them are going to be quite pissed. They say it's part of the job description. You make people laugh, hopefully you make them think, and frequently you make them angry.

The plus side is I get to draw cartoons for a living. When people hear that, their first response is often "So, what do you do with the rest of your day?" That usually has me spending the rest of my day explaining why the cartoon is what I do with the rest of my day. Hopefully the pages of this book will more fully explain what I do with the rest of my day.

A LITTLE HISTORY

My connections to The Herald run deep and predate me. When my father was a kid growing up in Halifax, he earned money as a paperboy delivering both papers, The Chronicle-Herald and The Mail-Star. He delivered 40 papers in the morning, 80 papers in the afternoon. Uphill, both ways, in a snowstorm, every day. That's what I'm told.

When I was a kid growing up in Antigonish in the '70s, The Herald arrived on our doorstep every day. For both of us, throughout that period and before, Bob Chambers was the editorial cartoonist for The Herald. I remember becoming aware of Chambers when I was about 12, getting hooked on his daily cartoon, and suddenly having a reason to read the paper. I also remember the feeling of disappointment when his final cartoon appeared only two years later. It was a caricature of his "little man" (a "John Q. Public" icon that he was both known for and identified with) riding off into a sunset marked "retirement." That ended over 40 years of daily cartoons by a talented, funny and humble gentleman whose work had made him a household name across the province.

Baseball was huge in Halifax in the '40s and '50s, and in late September 1946, the Halifax and District league was holding a big playoff game between Halifax and Truro at Wanderers Grounds downtown. Bob Chambers was in the crowd, enjoying the excitement and thinking about his next day's cartoon.

The game was deadlocked in extra innings and the bases were loaded. On an errant play, with a runner coming in from third base, the catcher missed the throw at the plate. A wide-eyed eight-year-old boy was standing in the crowd on the sidelines, and as the ball rolled nearby, a voice from behind the boy said "Why don't you get the ball, kid?" Obediently, the boy rushed out onto the field to snag the loose ball. Peaches Ruven, manager of the Truro team, bolted out after the boy to keep the ball in play as the opposing catcher also ran for the ball. They collided, the catcher was knocked out, and the opposing coach attacked Peaches Ruven, triggering a brawl. The crowd stormed the field, resulting in a riotous melee and the eventual cancellation of the game. The whole thing was captured in a Chambers cartoon which appeared in The Herald the next day. The boy was my dad, and that cartoon is still a subject of great pride and mirth in my family.

The Halifax Mail, September 30, 1946

Chambers drew his first cartoon for The Halifax Chronicle in 1923. It was about separation—Nova Scotia from the rest of Canada. He made $2.50 per cartoon, which, ironically, is exactly the same amount I made in my first cartooning job, drawing for the Antigonish weekly, The Casket, at the age of 14. (The fact that I got paid the same amount 50 years later probably says more about the relative value of the art than the long-term stability of the Canadian dollar, but then I'm no economist.) What possessed me to go to the local paper and ask for a job at the age of 14, I'm not sure. It may have been that playing street hockey wasn't paying the bills. Whatever it was, I suddenly found myself doing a weekly cartoon for the local paper. For the record, when this is all over, I hope to resume my street hockey career.

Bob Chambers had been retired for more than 10 years by the time I was hired full-time at The Herald. He was a small man I always looked up to. I got to know him as a friend and used to go visit him once or twice a year, usually around Christmastime, always packing a bottle of rum for the occasion. We'd sit and talk about the business, the people, and the fact that you can still drink rum in your 90s. There is life after retirement.

Things had changed so much, even in the short time since Bob had retired. One day I stopped by his place after work with a photocopy of the next day's cartoon. Bob looked at the piece of paper quizzically and asked, "What's this?"

I said, "It's a photocopy."

"A photocopy?"

"Yes, you take your original drawing, put it face down on the machine, press a button, and a copy comes out on another piece of paper."

"*Witchcraft*," he said.

My first definitively political cartoon was published when I was 15. It was a satirical poke at a local and very popular Antigonish MLA by the name of Bill Gillis. I've included the cartoon here at the expense of whatever personal and professional pride I may have. This was my… um, minimalist period. I remember entering one of those comic book contests around that time… you know: "Draw Sparky and you could be on your way to art school." Never heard back.

Spectator, August 1977

Gillis was the young incumbent, defending his first term as MLA. In the 30-plus years since then, I have gone from seeing my targets as mostly wrinkled old politicians, to actually being older, myself, than some of those I satirize. Ouch. That may be in part why, when Bill Gillis passed away in 2009, something felt to me like it had come full circle. The following is a cartoon and accompanying column I did at the time, in an effort to articulate that feeling.

Bill Gillis:
My first victim

My first published political cartoon was a send-up of my MLA, Bill Gillis. It was 1977, I was a Grade 10 student at Antigonish Regional High School, and after a year of drawing weekly cartoons on high school events for the local newspaper "The Casket", I had been lured away by upstart publisher Lauchie Chisholm to work for his new weekly, "The Spectator".

Incumbent MLA Gillis was about to be challenged in the upcoming provincial election by Tory candidate and former St. F.X. football coach Don Loney. Lauchie asked me to draw Bill Gillis dressed up in football gear, running to catch a football labelled "Antigonish riding," unaware that linebacker Don Loney stood poised to crush him before the catch. I was more interested in street hockey than politics back then and was more than happy to draw whatever my new boss wanted, and so my first truly political cartoon was published. A few weeks later, I received a warm and gracious letter in the mail from Dr. Gillis, commending me on my cartoon, offering substantially more praise than I deserved, and concluding with "… and I assure you, I intend to catch the ball and win the game." And win he did. Election after election, for nearly 30 years.

Receiving a personal letter from Bill Gillis was not unusual. In fact, if you lived in his riding, it would be more unusual to not receive a letter or some form of communication from him, whether it was congratulations, condolences, or to deal with an issue or help work out a problem. He was a politician who made a point of keeping in touch with his constituents. He was a humble individual who worked hard, was respected across party lines, and seemed to be in politics for all the right reasons. He was known among friends and journalists as "one-beer-Bill," an acknowledgment of his commitment to moderation despite the social nature of his job. He had a reputation for frugality and a weakness for Pizza Hut pizza.

Years later, working for The Chronicle Herald, I went on to draw many more cartoons of Bill Gillis throughout his career as an MLA. The last time I spoke with him, I was having supper with my wife Peggy and our kids at a Pizza Hut on Barrington Street. There was a leadership void at the time after the resignation of Dr. John Savage. Gillis was the most respected and senior MLA in the party, and I asked him whether he was considering a run at the leadership. He said he personally felt that if he ran for premier, he was crossing a line where he would need to put his job ahead of his family, something he was not prepared to do.

Political cartoonists rarely view politicians in a kind light, but Bill Gillis commanded respect and carried himself with integrity to the end. Perhaps there are some things you can take with you.

~Bruce MacKinnon

August 18, 2009

In the years after working for The Casket and The Spectator, I went from doing crazy and probably illegal cartoons for my high school newspaper to doing stuff I can't seem to remember for my university newspaper, The Xaverian, and eventually freelancing for various publications from here to Calgary.

The first time I went to The Herald looking for a job, in the summer of 1983, I was between semesters at the Nova Scotia College of Art and Design. I brought some examples of my cartoons in to show the managing editor at the time, Ken Foran. He didn't throw me out on my butt, which I took as a positive sign, but he didn't offer me Chambers' job right off the bat either. "Chambers was an institution here." That was something I'd hear a lot. I think it meant they weren't looking for a new institution just yet.

He sent me across the newsroom to talk to the editor of the weekend insert, The Nova Scotian. That editor was Jane Purves. If the name sounds familiar, there's good reason. Jane and I would cross paths in many different ways over the years that followed.

She was the first Herald editor to publish my work. After doing my first political cartoon for her, she asked if I could do non-political stuff—gag cartoons or strip cartoons as they call them. I was also working as a house painter that summer, so I did one gag cartoon a week for a month or so and then lost interest. Pulling jokes out of a hat has never felt as natural to me as doing political satire, so I gave up on the strip cartoons. Still, I like to tell my kids I started out as a stripper.

Jane eventually moved up the ranks at The Herald to become the first female managing editor at a major daily Canadian newspaper. Now she was the big cheese. When a cartoon was being axed for whatever reason, I often had to drop the gloves with Jane. Sometimes she was on my side, sometimes she was the heavy. We had more than a few heated arguments. Throughout, she was always fair, open-minded, and professional. That's what I'm told.

From here, most Nova Scotians know the story. Jane left the Herald in 1999 and to my total shock, bewilderment, and, well… glee…she ran for the Tories in the next provincial election. Against the odds, she not only won, but instantly became a cabinet minister in John Hamm's newly formed minority government.

Suddenly my old boss was my new target. There are people who fantasize for years about this situation. As if that weren't enough, Jane ended up in two of the most high-profile cabinet positions, first as Minister of Health, then Education. I was looking at my former boss in a whole new light. Picture a dunk tank and you're standing there with a limitless supply of, um…balls.

I have always liked and respected Jane Purves, as do most people who really know her. That said, business is business. I did a pile of cartoons on Jane during her time with the Hamm government. I like to think that, like her, I was tough but fair. Well, tough anyway.

August 23, 2001

Back to 1983. After a summer of painting houses and doing a few freelance cartoons for The Herald, I was back at NSCAD, studying design. My wife and I were newlyweds. Somehow, she got pregnant. I finished the school year and got a job at a local design firm, but also revisited The Herald to check on that "institution" position. I got my toe just a little further in the door when they agreed to try me in the editorial cartoon spot on a weekly basis. My first Herald editorial cartoon was on one of those perennially controversial issues—the seal hunt—involving then-minister of fisheries John Leefe.

In the interests of another "full circle" moment, I'm also including my most recent seal hunt cartoon, published just recently. Plus ça change.

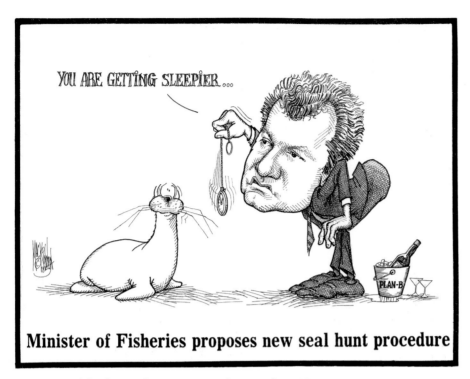

Minister of Fisheries proposes new seal hunt procedure

First Herald editorial cartoon, John Leefe, 1985

May 7, 2009

So now it's 1985. I'm Mr. Mom, looking after our newborn daughter, Robyn, while freelancing cartoons and design work out of my home. After just over a year of doing a cartoon a week, getting a few axed, and learning a few lessons about the difference between working for a "family newspaper" versus one of those subversive campus periodicals, I approached The Herald again. By this time, I suppose I'd pretty much worn them down. Ken Foran took me up to see the publisher, Graham Dennis, who seemed very satisfied that I was a homegrown lad and graciously welcomed me aboard.

The next few years were a bit of a learning curve. In those days, boundaries were everywhere, sacred cows mooed through the newsroom, and cartoons got axed almost as a matter of course. I think I was viewed partly as a curiosity, partly as a concern…like something from the Shubenacadie Wildlife Park that had been let loose in the building. People would come by and stare into my cage. Sometimes they'd ignore the sign and try to feed me.

Whenever I did a cartoon that crossed the line, or one of the many lines, I'd end up in the office with Ken Foran and usually at least one other senior editor, in a good cop/bad cop scenario. Actually it was more of a bad cop/bad cop scenario. I'd frequently end up leaving with my day's work in the trash, my knuckles broken and maybe later a horse's head in my bed. Okay, sometimes it was a cat. Okay I'm making that stuff up, but you get the idea.

Ken was a big, burly man with red hair which more or less matched his facial complexion. He always looked like he was about to explode, though he never did, at least at me. He was decent and respectful and we got along well. It may be that he also saw me as having the potential to explode, or at least I had to be handled that way. In any case, I will always owe him for seeing something of value in my work, back when he or anyone would have had to look pretty hard.

Things were starting to heat up in Halifax print journalism. There was fresh competition from the upstart Daily News and a new scandal sheet called Frank magazine. A pattern began to emerge where whenever one of my cartoons got pulled, the story would turn up in Frank magazine. I had an idea who was responsible, but never knew for sure. There were certain regulars who would drop by my workspace through the day to rattle my cage, and I had a feeling one in particular might be leaking details of the pulled cartoons. It wasn't all bad, in that it probably had the effect of loosening my leash a bit in the long run, but I was aware it probably looked like I was leaking the news myself—something I was concerned might cost me my job.

Over the years, things gradually changed and more of a mutual trust developed between my keepers and me. I kept pushing my luck, but I got sent to the penalty box less often. When it did happen, the reasons were either legal or matters of taste. The most recent rejection was an airport security concept—something to do with priests, pat-downs and full body scanners that was doomed from the start. You get to know where the danger zones are, but you're strangely drawn to them anyway.

There was one I submitted on Bush's missile defence plan a few years back which involved a nuclear missile protruding from a beaver's…um…end. Terry O'Neil, the newsroom boss of the day, made his terms clear. "You can have it in his ear, up his nose…any orifice but that one…"

My immediate supervisor from the beginning has been Editor-in-Chief Bob Howse—a talented writer and a funny, affable guy who truly deserves an award for endurance, in being my baby-sitter for 25 years. He would often go to bat for me on a touchy cartoon. If he struck out, he'd come back to my office with his head lowered, glumly announcing "The reaper is here…"

I've been lucky to work with people like Bob and others in the editorial department whom I trust to tell me if a cartoon works, is funny or unpublishable for whatever reason. If a cartoon gets killed now, it's almost always in the idea stage. It's probably better that way. It saves a lot of pointless work and gives me another shot at getting published that day. On the downside, I don't get to the pub as early as I used to.

WE GET LETTERS

Throughout my tenure with The Chronicle Herald I've done cartoons that have gotten me in varying degrees of hot water. This section will feature some of the more notable cartoons in that category.

In 2008, it got particularly weird. There were a couple of incidents, the most significant of which started on April 17, 2008, when a front-page story appeared in The Herald with the headline, "I Want Millions!" It involved a development in the case of the now-infamous "Toronto 18," a group of men accused of, among other things, plotting to blow up the Parliament buildings in Ottawa and behead the prime minister (something I wasn't necessarily *entirely* opposed to).

The prosecution had announced a stay of charges against one of the men in the case. He had been accused of attending a terrorist training camp, something which is now a proven fact and a matter of court record by way of evidence admitted in the convictions and guilty pleas of many of his co-accused.

His wife was a former Nova Scotian who had converted to Islam. Her public reaction to the stay was to say she planned to sue Canada for millions in damages. She even mused about using the proceeds of the lawsuit to buy Alexander Graham Bell's family estate and mansion in Baddeck, Cape Breton. This was, at best, a little premature considering a prosecutorial stay does not mean a defendant is out of the woods, but only that the charges, which can be reactivated, have been put aside for the time being.

Stories like this require more research and due diligence than a story on the latest tax hikes or cabinet shuffles. While it's not necessarily the type of subject matter I'm comfortable with, it demands the same scrutiny and debate as any other story, perhaps more so, given what is at stake.

I had a contact in the legal community in Toronto who was very familiar with this case, so I gave him a call. I told him I had a cartoon concept for this story and wanted to know if it was fair and safe in his legal opinion. His first response was to laugh out loud (not always a good sign). He was very helpful in explaining the facts and reasons for the stay. In Canada it is very difficult to prosecute a large group under the same charges. The prosecution had chosen to focus on the major players.

After hashing things out with my legal contact, I called Dan Leger, The Herald's director of news content. I explained the cartoon and the rationale behind it. His response was that it was a hard-hitting cartoon (the term he used was "an ice pick to the head"), and he supported it 100 percent. In it went.

The cartoon I came up with showed the woman in what was essentially a replication of the front-page photo from the day before, with my punchline added.

April 18, 2008

At first there was minimal response—a couple of letters of complaint and a similar amount of positive feedback. Then nothing, until two weeks later when I got word that someone from a relatively new group called "The Centre for Islamic Development" had been on CBC radio decrying the cartoon as racist. The next day, I was notified that I was under police investigation as a result of a complaint from the same group and further, that the group had launched a human rights complaint against me. Hmm.

The news began making headlines across the country and the following day I awoke to a story in my own paper stating that I was being investigated under Section 318 of the Criminal Code, which deals with hate propaganda. That section says: "Every one who advocates or promotes genocide is guilty of an indictable offence and liable to imprisonment for a term not exceeding five years."

It's not every morning you wake up and read in your newspaper that you're being investigated for the promotion of genocide, not to mention facing prison time. Mom would have been so proud…

In nearly 25 years of drawing cartoons for The Herald, I have established a fairly consistent record of attacking racism and defending minority rights. Outside my work, those who know me know that I don't aspire to much beyond playing guitar and drinking good quality craft beer now and then. I really don't think I could fit genocide into that schedule even if I wanted to. That would require some commitment, I would imagine, though I haven't looked into it.

Within a matter of weeks I was informed that the police wouldn't be pursuing charges. The human rights complaint, however, remained outstanding and, I was told, could drag on for years.

Dan Leger eventually managed to set up a meeting with representatives from the Centre for Islamic Development in an attempt to hear their concerns and offer them space in the paper to air their views. During the meeting, the group pulled out a few other cartoons I had done which they felt showed an anti-Muslim bias, including one from more than a year earlier. The cartoon was in reference to a news story about a highly controversial "Holocaust conference" in Iran, at which a former American KKK grand wizard named David Duke was invited to speak. Here you had a white supremacist speaking at a mostly Muslim conference in Iran on the "myth" of the Holocaust.

Strange bedfellows, to say the least. The irony was irresistible. I drew a cartoon that I felt addressed issues of both racism and sexism. This group apparently did not appreciate my approach.

December 14, 2006

It was unfortunate that in researching my work, the group from the Centre for Islamic Development seemed to overlook any cartoons I had done that defended Muslims or promoted minority rights over the years, including several I had done around the same period defending Maher Arar, a Muslim man who had been deported to Syria and detained for over a year.

In the Toronto 18 case, the differences were stark and have become even clearer in the time that has since passed. Eleven of the original eighteen have been convicted of terrorism offences. Five others, including the individual referred to in the cartoon, have been deemed by the courts to be a threat to commit future terrorist acts and have signed peace bonds that place them under strict conditions and oversight. This was not a Boy Scout camp. Many of these men had very real plans to wreak havoc on Canadian soil in the name of Islamic fundamentalism and are now serving lengthy prison terms.

To this date, I haven't been contacted by anyone from the Human Rights Commission, although within a year of the original complaint I received second-hand information that the commission had dropped the matter.

All this coincided with a growing national debate about the role of human rights commissions and their increasing intervention in the right to free speech. My case was cited in columns and blogs across the country and lumped in with other cases being fought at the same time by journalists such as Mark Steyn of Maclean's and Ezra Levant, publisher of the now-defunct Western Standard. Again, strange bedfellows…at least for me. On one hand, I was disturbed to learn how far beyond their original mandate human rights commissions had begun to reach. On the other hand, I was equally uncomfortable finding myself being defended by voices from the extreme right. Hmm. Time to pour a beer and play some guitar.

❊ ❊ ❊

Another 2008 cartoon that dealt with racial issues also turned out to be the gift that kept on giving. In January of that year it was clear that Barack Obama had a promising shot at becoming the first African American to win the presidency. I saw this as a very positive development and had a feeling I might be drawing him a lot more in the near future.

The term "White House" seemed like a fairly inescapable metaphor for the centuries of white male domination of the U.S. presidency, especially in the face of an emerging black presidential candidate. The resulting cartoon was what I still consider to be an obvious concept, probably too obvious.

January 6, 2008

I didn't think much of it at the time. It was my first Obama caricature, and I didn't get a good likeness. Maybe there was something about the gesture, maybe his look was too stern, I don't know. In any case, in it went. As with any cartoon involving racial issues, it got some response, again from both sides. There was only one negative call initially, from an American expat, who, while very reasonable and understanding, seemed to be quite certain Americans wouldn't take it the way I'd intended.

Americans are big on their icons, and the very idea that the name of one of their greatest symbols might have to change if a black man were elected president went to the heart of their racial insecurities, satire or not. I explained the cartoon was supposed to represent a positive message about racial progress in America, and people couldn't seriously think anyone was about to change the name of the White House. Furthermore, so what if they did? It's just a name. It's just a colour.

That didn't win this expat over. He also thought I'd drawn Obama's ears too big. Like I've never done that to anyone before.

I didn't hear anything more until weeks later when the cartoon appeared on the Association of American Editorial Cartoonists' website. Not long after that, it started circulating widely online throughout the U.S., and I began receiving more and more email responses from Americans. Initially, most were from indignant conservatives who admitted they would never vote for Obama but felt offended on his behalf.

I responded to some, but the volume of mail gradually became overwhelming and the content more and more bizarre. The cartoon started popping up everywhere south of the border with racially charged propaganda added. It seemed a few people with racist agendas had appropriated the cartoon and defaced it for their own misinformation campaigns.

Throughout the summer of 2008, I received dozens of emails a week from Americans on the defaced version of this cartoon, as the presidential election race raged on. The story of the altered cartoon made headlines in Canada and the U.S.

At a Republican convention in Texas, a vendor attempted to sell buttons that read in stark, black-and-white lettering, "If Obama is President…will we still call it the White House?" The vendor claimed it was inspired by the cartoon, which prompted a columnist from the Fort Worth Star-Telegram to track me down and interview me about it. He was sympathetic to the original cartoon and as angry as I was about the distortion of it. I was happy to have a voice down there to tell the story from my perspective.

The whole experience was quite an eye-opener and an interesting study in human behaviour. When I first started working for The Herald, it didn't take long to figure out that cartoons that deal with race elicit strong, emotional, and often irrational responses. You realize a need to be extremely clear, with nothing even slightly open to interpretation. This does not necessarily make for a good editorial cartoon. On the other hand, you can only smoke so many exploding cigars before you feel the urge to avoid the subject matter altogether, which is wrong. It's okay to talk about race. Really. We have to.

※ ※ ※

In 2005, I did a cartoon in response to a front-page news story about my old college residence. When the cartoon sparked a considerable backlash, I felt some context might be in order. The following is a column I wrote to address the feedback, along with the original cartoon.

MacIsaac Hall and Me

When I told my father, a long-time history professor at St. F.X., that I planned to stay on campus during my first year at X, he said "Apply for MacPherson." It wasn't a suggestion. Back in the early '80s MacPherson was known as a quieter residence where good students could focus on their studies. When the letter came back that MacPherson was full but I had been accepted at MacIsaac ("Mac" to most Xaverians), my father's response was "No damn way." I have to admit I was intrigued and fairly excited that this residence had such a fearsome reputation for wildness that my father was this adamant that I stay somewhere else. The issue was moot in the end because I was paying my own way and I think we both wanted me to stay on campus. Mac it was.

So it was with a great deal of interest I read the story on the front page of last Wednesday's Herald about the most recent controversy surrounding the "Burmac Cup," an annual hockey game put on by the residents of MacIsaac and Burke Houses to raise money for "X-Project," a mentoring and tutoring program for minority children in the Antigonish area. The game has traditionally been a fun—if sometimes rowdy—outlet for the rivalry between the two residences. It's also been one of the university's more successful fundraisers.

The incident that sparked the news stories at first read like the classic college prank. Students sneak in to the rival residence under the cover of darkness and tape up some lewd posters to greet residents in the morning—in this case the female occupants of that wing of Burke, a co-ed residence.

As I read the story I wasn't aware it had also been the lead story on the ATV evening news and was making similar waves throughout the local media. My first thought was "Wow, Mac made the news. Cool!" The twist was the nature of the posters and the effect they had. There were cries from on campus that the posters went beyond vulgar, were highly offensive to women, and

intended to incite violence. It was hard to get an accurate read from the description in the story, as the only poster singled out was described as a drawing of a female, naked from the waist down, with a somewhat phallic piece of paper maché work attached, and a crude caption (not quoted in the story). As my wife Peggy (also an X alumna) read the story, her reaction was to wonder what all the fuss was about. In the absence of any more detail than a description of a lewd drawing, my reaction was generally the same. The response from the university brass was more decisive, and the much-anticipated hockey game was cancelled.

I knew my old Mac mates would be waiting for a cartoon reaction from me. The concept I came up with showed some generic male students entering one door of MacIsaac and coming out the other end as monkeys.

My feeling was the cartoon worked in either case. If the incident was as serious an offence as was claimed by some, then the perpetrators deserved the suggestion that they were devolving. If it was just a prank that went a bit too far, then the cartoon should have been received in the same spirit as that which delivered the prank—a good-natured poke, something which any Mac resident I ever knew would have been just as happy to take as to give. (For those who didn't read the fine print under my signature, the cartoon was unabashedly signed "Former resident, 4th Mac.")

Mac was where I got my basic training in irreverent humour. Were I still 19 and living there, I would likely be thumping my chest at my residence having made the provincial paper. It could be that even after 20 years in the workforce I'm not yet far enough removed from my university days to take things that seriously. Frankly, as I was drawing the cartoon I kept picturing myself drawing it on the residence bathroom wall. (Yes Mr. President, it was I who was responsible for most of the graffiti in that middle stall back in '81–'82. There. I admit it.)

Since the original story broke, subsequent reports have put the incident in a constantly changing light. A story the next day had female Burke residents, the purported victims, complaining it all had been blown out of proportion. A more recent story on the weekend revealed that the first two students to confess to being part of the stunt were actually women, which put my knee-jerk assumption of male culpability off the rails. (Mac was a male-only residence when I lived there, back when dinosaurs roamed the Earth.) It also undermines the theory put forth by some that the infraction was motivated by misogyny. Now, with the possibility of charges being laid against at least two very upset and remorseful female students, it certainly appears it might be time for everybody to take a deep breath and step back a bit.

February 3, 2005

Many decent individuals and exceptional students have passed through the doors of MacIsaac Hall over the years. I shared a year with some of those students, as well as others who, like me, were filling in time, still trying to figure out what they really wanted to do with their lives. It was one of the best and most memorable years of my life. Despite incidents such as this, which will occur when young people are learning where the boundaries are, I'm extremely proud of my time at MacIsaac and neither this incident nor the cartoon change that in any way.

* * *

During her tenure as Canada's Governor General, Adrienne Clarkson had been criticized for her ballooning travel budget. On her retirement in September 2005 the following cartoon and responding letter were published. I was trashed by Farley Mowat. I still can't believe it. I'm finally somebody.

September 23, 2005

Claire and
FARLEY MOWAT

TO;   The Editor, The Halifax Chronicle Herald

          Your cartoon of September 23rd of departing
Governor General Adrienne Clarkson was an insult to
her and to the office of Governor General and a
disgrace to your newspaper.   The implication that
she has been squandering taxpayers' money on high
living and luxury travel bears the spiteful ring
of ignorance.   You should well know that the
Governor General, travelling as Canada's Head Of
State, must go first class as does every other
Head of State the world over.   You must know that
she does not choose or set her travel itinerary
but that this is done by the Canadian Department
of Foreign Affairs.   You must be aware that the
arrangements for her official travels are made
by that department, which sets the standards for
them and pays for them on behalf of the Canadian
people.

          Shame on you for a sleazy denigration of
an honourable woman who had made a significant,
dedicated and imaginative contribution to Canada
during the six years she has been our Governor
General.

                              Farley and Claire Mowat

✳✳✳

In 2004, the following cartoon raised the hackles of some Bush supporters and drew some letters. Still, I liked it and overall, it was well received, so I included it in the "Best of" year-end page. That prompted a bigger pile of letters. What, were you people all on vacation when it first came out? A few months later it won second prize in a world cartoon competition and so was published again. More letters. *Enough* already.

MISSING LINK

July 18, 2004

January 8, 1998

What I remember most about this cartoon is that it was a bad day for Jane Purves. It was January 1998 and Jane was my managing editor. Hockey czar Alan Eagleson had just been sentenced to 18 months in prison for fraud. At the same time, Graham James, the notorious junior hockey coach convicted of sexually assaulting his young players, was serving his own sentence. These were two high-profile cases and though drastically different in nature, both shared the theme of victimized hockey players. Seemed like a natural combination, though I was fully aware the subject matter would be hard for some to stomach. I did the pencil sketch and, anticipating a day's work going down in flames, went out to the newsroom to place it directly before the likely executioner.

As I remember it, Jane had just come from one of those meetings where journalism and business clash, and though I don't remember the exact circumstances, she looked like she had lost a battle. I showed her the cartoon, she shook her head wearily and said, "Oh what the hell…things can't get any worse today…"

September 6, 1998

This cartoon probably generated more mail than I'd ever received before. When Swiss Air 111 crashed into the waters off Peggy's Cove in 1998, it was one of the biggest air disasters in history and it happened right in our backyard. The story was horrific. Normally, plane crashes are not something I consider for subject matter, but in this case the story was so huge and so local, there was no way to ignore it.

The image I came up with had a solemn tone and was intended as a tribute to the fishermen who went out after the crash to aid in the rescue effort—an effort that sadly ended up as a morbid cleanup.

People are sensitive about death and tragedy at the best of times, but it needs to be understood that an editorial cartoon can be a statement, a tribute—it doesn't always have to be considered a joke. For some, there's an assumption that equates any cartoon, even editorial, with "Garfield" or something that belongs on the comics page.

The letters and phone calls of outrage came pouring in. As if that weren't enough, a local talk radio show host spent a week on the cartoon, encouraging listeners to call in and voice their outrage. I had difficulty understanding how people could so misread the intent of the cartoon, but in retrospect I think the shock of the tragedy was so great that they simply needed a lightning rod to vent their anger, and I was it. It was a bit dispiriting at the time. I'm fine if people disagree with my point of view, but if they simply misinterpret the cartoon, I see it as failure on my part to communicate the message effectively.

After the first week or so of relentlessly negative fallout, things turned around and there came a backlash to the backlash, where an even greater number of letters came streaming in defending the cartoon. That was at least some vindication and gave me back a little faith that I wasn't completely out of my mind when I first thought of the idea.

Gunplay in Spryfield and the antics of the notorious Melvin "crime family" prompted this cartoon that played on the Sopranos logo. My hockey pals from Spryfield got a big kick out of it. Unfortunately, no one else from Spryfield did. (Note to self: Don't mess with Spryfield.)

November 19, 2008

ABOUT FACE

My favourite part of this job has always been drawing caricatures. I put myself through art college by doing portraits and caricatures in a Halifax shopping mall. That was as much boot camp for editorial cartooning as anything. Having to draw on the clock, often with a crowd watching over your shoulder, teaches you a lot about meeting deadlines. And bladder control.

Some of the cartoons in this section were illustrations for features rather than actual editorial cartoons. They might not all be cutting-edge political satire, but they made my pencil stand up.

Sarah Palin

August 23, 2009

Neil Young
November 30, 2008

Conan O'Brien
January 24, 2010

Paul Martin
April 8, 2005

Jack Layton
April 26, 2005

Juno host Pamela Anderson

April 2006

Dutch Mason
September 15, 2005

Karlheinz Schreiber
December 5, 2007

Brian Mulroney
February 29, 2008

Paris Hilton

June 10, 2007

Sidney Crosby
August 2009

ECMA hosts The Trailer Park Boys (plus big winner George Canyon)
February 2007

Dave Carroll

September 24, 2009

A DAY IN THE LAUGH

The question I get asked most frequently, whether on the street, at social functions, or during police interrogations is "Where do you get your ideas?" The answer: from my idea jar. When I wake up in the morning, the first thing I do is check the idea jar. If there's nothing in it, I pour myself three or four stiff drinks, read the paper and then check the idea jar again. If there's still nothing there, I poke some holes in the lid to make sure I'm not killing the ideas before they can grow.

Actually, most days it's a bit more complicated than that. Usually I start with coffee, then the paper. I have a scratch pad for ideas. At the top of the page I always write "Today," so I won't forget what day it is. Then I jot down the stories that are the most likely candidates for the day's cartoon. Then I check the idea jar again. If there's still nothing there, I take it out of the fridge and leave it in the sun for a while. Stuff grows better in the sun.

So I've had my coffee, read my paper and I'm sitting in my office with all the modern devices of communication around me. First thing I do is call Rocky. Rocky, whose nickname is Laurent Le Pierres, is the editorial writer and columnist who succeeded Jim Meek as my main sounding board. (Meek is the former editorial writer and columnist who left because he couldn't take my relentless interruptions and phone calls anymore.) The sounding board job isn't as glorious as it might sound. It entails getting sporadic and mostly incoherent calls from me throughout the day. I mumble about what I've read in the news and spew ideas that would otherwise embarrass me if I didn't have more lucid people to keep them from becoming public. The sounding board job doesn't pay much. Okay, it doesn't pay anything, but on the plus side, it's highly unrewarding.

I have two other sounding boards who receive much the same compensation. One is a very talented cartoonist on the West Coast by the name of Bob Krieger. As soon as Krieger wakes up, we have an email exchange that usually goes something like this:

"Hey. You awake?"

"No."

"I got nothin'. What've you got?"

"A headache and a pot of coffee."

After that we go back to our stewing pots and only poke our heads out if we need to argue about issues or see how an idea rates on the guffaw meter.

My other sounding board is my wife, Peggy. She has persevered with an open-minded, objective opinion for longer than anyone. She has also bailed me out with some pretty great ideas of her own over the years.

This brings me to another point. Of all the letters, emails, and phone calls I receive, probably the most common theme is contributed ideas. In recent years I've mostly had to stop replying to people who send these because I can't keep up. Sometimes people just want their issue addressed or their point of view heard, which is perfectly understandable. Sometimes the ideas sound like this: "So you draw Napoleon's army on one side facing a battalion of gay sumo wrestlers armed with chocolate éclairs, while a naked paraplegic with three breasts plays the accordion underwater…." On the one hand, it's very gratifying to know that people are engaged and want to be involved. On the other hand, it's hard to explain in a delicate way that I prefer to use my own concepts. If I take an idea from anybody, it's going to be my wife. But then I have to do the dishes, so it's a trade-off. Aside from that, and the odd time a friend like Rocky or Bob might toss me a bone, it's mostly just me and my idea jar. I prefer it that way.

If it's afternoon and I don't have an idea, I start to sweat. I check the idea jar. By now it's been in the sun too long so if there's an idea in there, it probably stinks. The longer I go without an idea, the more limited my options become. I've gone as late as 4:00 p.m. before coming up with a concept. Deadline is basically suppertime. At that point, drawing Napoleon's army is definitely out.

I usually start sketching in pencil. I rough out the design in loose blocks and shapes and then if necessary, I ransack my clippings or search the web for photo references of what or whomever I might need to draw. Once I flesh out the design and get the caricature right, I get the pens and start inking.

India ink is the reason I wear black almost all the time. Any clothes I have that aren't black have black ink stains on them. It only took me 15 years or so to figure out that wearing black would save me a lot of money on clothes.

After the inking is done and spills have been cleaned up, I send the cartoon in to Bev Dauphinee, my long-suffering letters page editor. She corrects my spelling and I get even by keeping her late.

Throughout the day I try to keep up with mail or phone calls while I draw, depending on the panic level of the hour. People call and write for all kinds of reasons. Often they want to give me an idea, sometimes they want to tell me they liked a cartoon, sometimes they want to tear a strip off me. A person's take on a given cartoon is often framed by their own ideology. Liberals accuse me of being a Tory, Tories accuse me of being a Liberal. Currently I'm not making any friends in the new NDP provincial government. Frequently I wonder if there's anyone left on the planet I have yet to alienate. If there is, I'm sure it's only a matter of time.

DEATHS IN THE FAMILY

There is almost no cartoon that elicits as much response as the dreaded "obit cartoon." I say dreaded because it creates a conundrum. It offers little in the way of political satire and can too easily become a facile, maudlin excuse to jerk tears. Still, when famous people die, it's often the biggest story of the day and an unavoidable subject for the cartoonist. The challenge is in finding an original way to deal with it so you can live with yourself in the morning.

The two most common obit cartoon clichés are the old "tear in the eye" (of whoever may be symbolically associated with the deceased), and the "St. Peter welcoming the deceased into heaven" (usually with some sort of sentimental gag attached). I have been shamefully guilty of both, though I've tried to present an original twist the few times I've done them.

When Ernie Coombs (a.k.a. Mr. Dressup) passed away more than a decade ago, the news broke late in the day after I had already submitted a cartoon on a different subject. The next day I had emails from readers, asking "Where's our Mr. Dressup cartoon?" Like many Canadians of my…um, vintage, I was a loyal Mr. Dressup follower as a kid. So I scratched my head for a bit and gave it some thought. The first idea that came to mind was to show his co-star puppets, Casey (yes…with a tear in his eye) hugging Finnegan. I ran the idea by my wife Peggy, my best friend and most reliable sounding board. "It's too maudlin," she said. Hmm. Peg's never wrong. That's what I'm told.

In a rare fit of independent thought, I decided to go with it anyway. The response was overwhelming. That cartoon remains one of the most talked-about I've ever done, something which probably speaks more to the sentimental attachment people have to Mr. Dressup than anything the cartoon offered.

Another cartoon that ranks on a similar scale in terms of response was when Theodor Seuss Geisel (a.k.a. Dr. Seuss) and legendary jazz pioneer Miles Davis passed away within days of each other. This time, the idea was actually Peg's suggestion: to have the two men standing on a cloud facing each other, Davis wearing his signature fedora, trumpet in hand, saying "So you're Dr. Seuss," and Dr. Seuss replying, "So you're the cat in the hat." That remains one of the coolest ideas I never thought of.

As popular as these cartoons tend to be, they can also be a minefield of sensitivity and emotion. When CBC broadcast journalist Barbara Frum succumbed to cancer in the early 1990s, I did a cartoon of her floating skyward, guided by an angel and inquiring, "Will He agree to an interview?" One of the first calls I fielded over that cartoon was from a member of the Frum family, who said they were touched by the tribute and wanted to know if they could purchase the original. Relieved and happy to oblige, I assured them I would send it ASAP, no charge. The next call I fielded was from a very angry woman in Cape Breton who didn't seem even slightly swayed by the fact that the Frums had asked for the original. Before she hung up she declared, "If that was my daughter I'd come right down there and break your neck!" Hmm.

All of the aforementioned obit cartoons have been republished in previous books so they aren't included here. The next few pages include more recent tribute cartoons from the past eight years. Please note I have done my best to maintain an original twist and avoid tear drops and pearly gates.

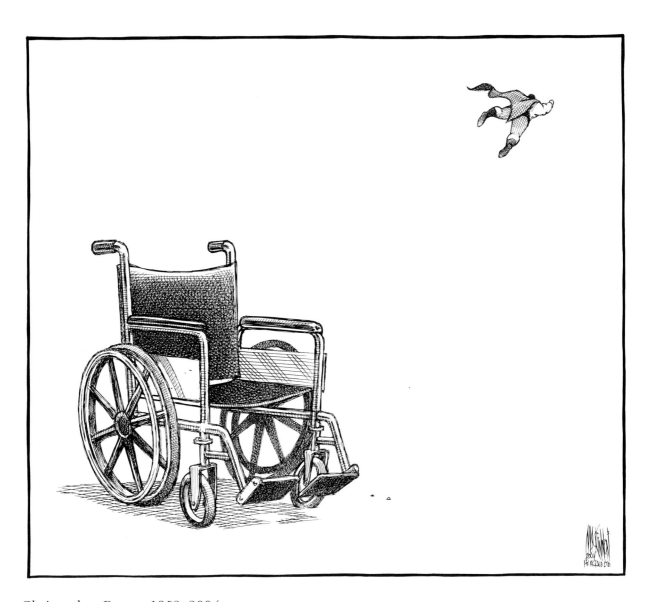

Christopher Reeve: 1952–2004

October 13, 2004

Ray Charles: 1930–2004

June 13, 2004

September 14, 2003

June 25, 2008

Robert Stanfield: 1914–2003

December 18, 2003

Howard Dill,
beloved local farmer
and world champion
pumpkin grower:
1934–2008

May 22, 2008

James Delorey,
a seven-year-old
Cape Breton boy
with autism, got
lost in the woods
along with his dog,
Chance, during a
severe snowstorm in
December 2009. He
was found after two
days, barely alive,
but passed away
shortly thereafter in
hospital.

December 9, 2009

WHAT HAVE YOU DONE FOR ME LATELY?

(CARTOONS FROM 2002–2009)

In an effort to avoid redundancy, I am avoiding the redundancy of republishing cartoons that have appeared in previous collections of my work. The following section contains cartoons not previously published in previous collections of my work, hence avoiding redundancy.

PROVINCIAL

Atlantic Jazz Fest, Stan Fest, and other summer music festivals wash over Nova Scotia

July 10, 2002

August 15, 2002

January 9, 2004

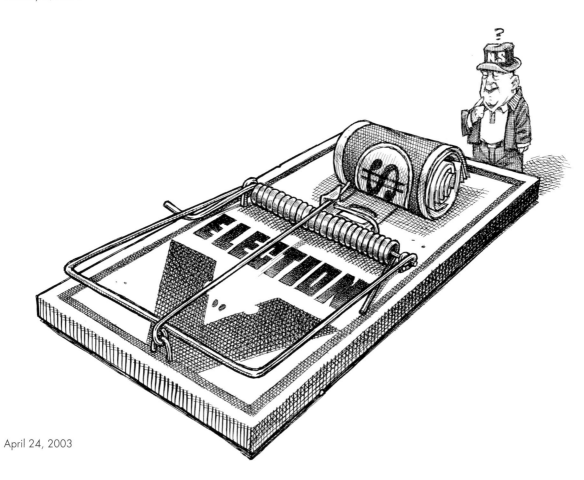

April 24, 2003

HAMM SANDWICH

John Hamm wins minority government

August 7, 2003

April 1, 2004

September 30, 2003

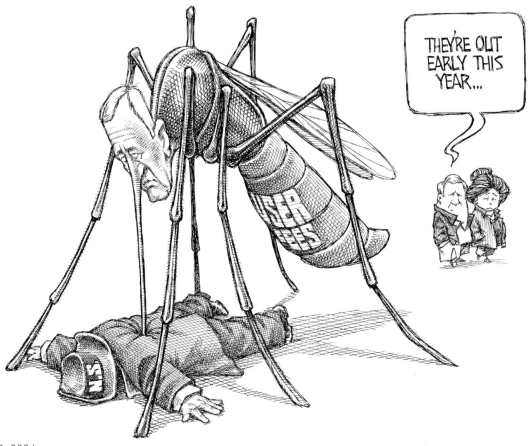

April 2, 2004

December 12, 2004

March 16, 2004

October 22, 2004

September 6, 2007

January 7, 2005

May 16, 2003

April 5, 2006

November 29, 2006

Problem-plagued
submarines
perpetually in
dry dock

May 1, 2009

June 12, 2007

October 8, 2008

January 16, 2009

Darrell Dexter elected first NDP Premier of Nova Scotia

June 11, 2009

More sex abuse scandals rock the Catholic church

October 4, 2009

October 25, 2009

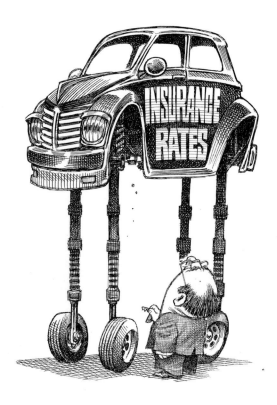

September 25, 2002

October 29, 2009

February 26, 2009

January 6, 2010

April 17, 2005

June 26, 2007

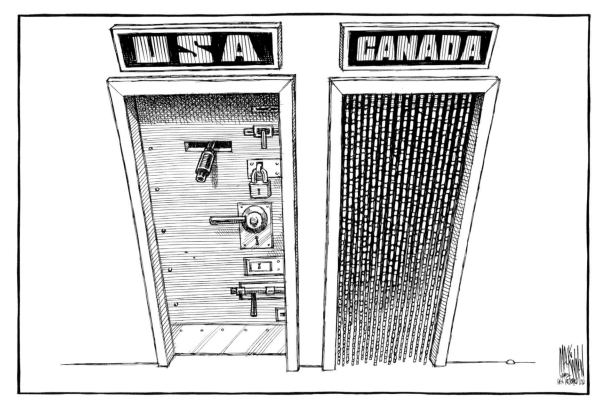

September 5, 2002

July 1, 2004

November 20, 2005

Beijing Summer Olympics

August 17, 2008

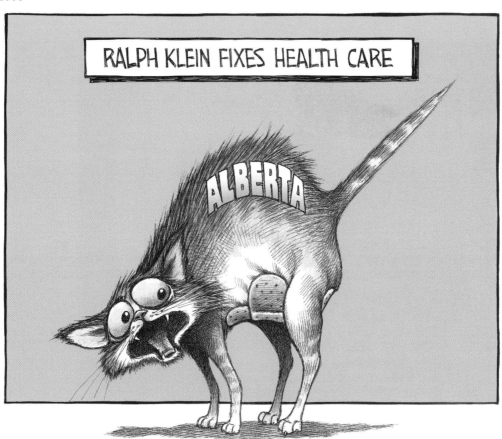

July 4, 2004

March 24, 2004

Tory election advertising "in and out" scheme evokes spectre of sponsorship scandal

April 23, 2008

February 18, 2005

May 2, 2004

May 28, 2004

June 4, 2002

November 21, 2003

May 27, 2004

PM Paul Martin
addresses the
nation regarding
the sponsorship
scandal

April 22, 2005

June 28, 2007

May 15, 2006

January 10, 2006

June 4, 2006

October 1, 2006

Peter MacKay receives a barrage of criticism after he is reported to have referred to ex-lover and former fellow Tory MP Belinda Stronach as his dog, in response to heckling from the opposition benches.

October 22, 2006

May 31, 2005

October 2, 2002

September 28, 2006

April 13, 2007

April 26, 2007

May 24, 2007

June 16, 2004

May 30, 2007

December 4, 2005

Gov. Gen. Michaelle Jean is recalled from a state visit in Europe to meet with Prime Minister Stephen Harper after the opposition parties form a coalition which threatens to bring down the government.

December 5, 2008

December 2, 2008

December 7, 2008

February 4, 2007

February 27, 2008

March 7, 2007

Top Mounties accused
of fraud involving the
RCMP pension and
insurance plans

April 1, 2007

January 27, 2008

March 11, 2009

January 31, 2008

January 9, 2008

January 10, 2008

May 2, 2008

October 23, 2008

January 21, 2010

May 28, 2008

October 18, 2007

November 26, 2008

October 17, 2008

October 26, 2006

September 23, 2008

August 14, 2009

April 23, 2009

September 14, 2008

February 22, 2009

Karla Homolka gives emotional interview after her release from prison

June 5, 2005

July 26, 2009

October 12, 2006

March 3, 2009

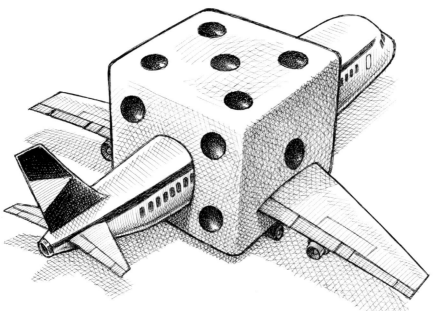

Volcanic ash in skies

April 20, 2010

December 10, 2009

May 31, 2009

INTERNATIONAL

August 28, 2005

April 4, 2004

April 9, 2004

March 30, 2003

January 20, 2004

June 6, 2003

May 18, 2004

October 27, 2005

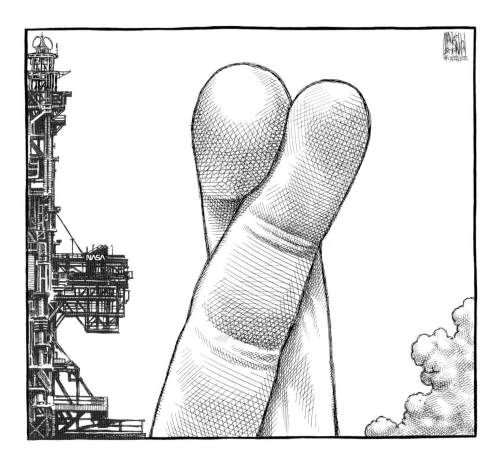

July 27, 2005

June 24, 2005

March 26, 2005

August 20, 2006

February 5, 2006

July 31, 2005

November 3, 2005

July 6, 2006

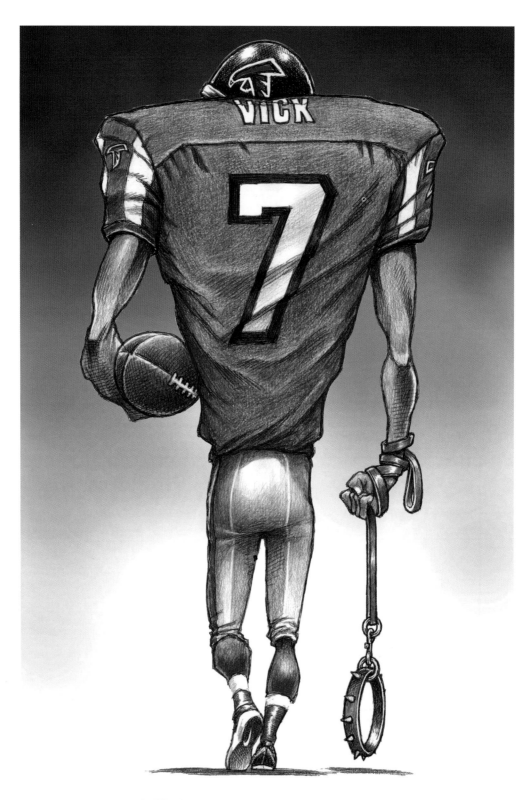

August 26, 2007

July 10, 2007

New York Yankees pitcher Cory Lidle crashes into a New York city skyscraper while piloting a small plane, raising questions about lax air traffic control regulations in post-9-11 New York.

October 13, 2006

September 21, 2007

September 9, 2007

October 19, 2008

November 20, 2008

February 11, 2009

MAMMALS IN TROUBLE

October 8, 2008

January 16, 2009

Sen. Ted Kennedy
backs Obama in
Democratic
leadership race

January 30, 2008

Obama elected
President

January 21, 2009

March 31, 2009

June 3, 2009

October 11, 2009

January 17, 2010

August 3, 2008

March 21, 2010

January 4, 2008

October 31, 2002